The Base Ball Player's Pocket Companion

Author: Anonymous

Publisher: Mayhew & Baker

"The Base Ball Player's Pocket Companion" is a significant piece of baseball literature, dating back to the mid-19th century. It was one of the earliest books to formalize the rules and strategies of baseball, making it a cornerstone document in the history of the game. This guidebook was likely intended for players and enthusiasts of the era, offering insights into playing techniques, rules of the game, and guidelines for setting up matches and teams.

1859 Edition

Republished 2024 by Baseball Classics™

Foreword by Baseball Classics Founder

DEAN PATINO

Copyright © 2024 by Baseball Classics

All rights reserved.

The original The Base Ball Player's Pocket Companion by Henry Chadwick, is in the public domain. All original additions, including illustrations and written content, are copyright © 2024 by Baseball Classics and may not be reproduced in any form without written permission from the publisher or author, except permitted by United States copyright law.

Cover Art by Baseball Classics

Republished by Baseball Classics 2024

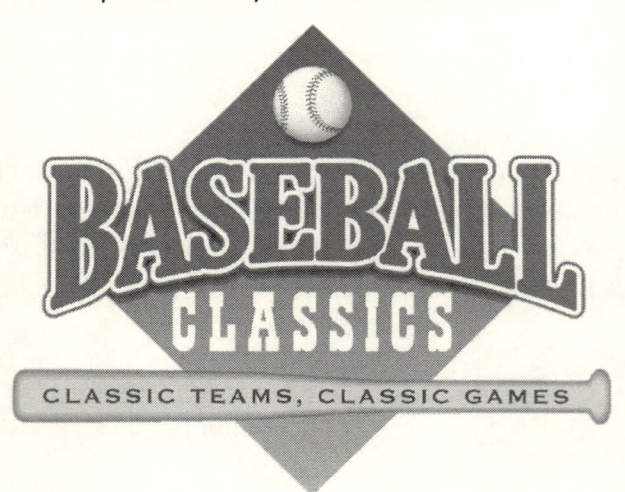

Baseball Classics © 2024
P.O. Box 911056
St. George, Utah
84791

www.BaseballClassics.com

Dedication

This book is dedicated to all those who created, formalized, played, umpired, scored, cheered, published, and supported the origins and adoption of Baseball.

Foreword

The first full published book on Baseball, is "The Base Ball Player's Pocket Companion" in 1859 by Henry Chadwick, according to reputable sources such as the Society For American Baseball Research (SABR), Public Broadcasting System (PBS), HistoryofInformation.com, and archive.org.

Mayhew & Baker were publishers, booksellers, and stationers. The author is anonymous, though one could speculate Officers of Massachusetts Association of Base Ball Players and those representing New York had input.

It was written after much controversy on how Baseball was to be played where it evolved in Massachusetts and grew to become a major regional sport expanding play primarily in New York, Philadelphia, and New Jersey.

As a result, two sets of "Base Ball" rules formed; one from Massachusetts and the other from New York.

The Massachusetts rules diagram the field in the shape of a square with bases 60 feet apart using wooden stakes as bases, rather than a diamond as played by the New York rules with bases spread 90 feet apart using sand or sawdust filled "bases" with a flat circular iron plate, painted or enameled white.

Ultimately, the New York set of rules became the standard. During the Civil War, baseball was played in camps by the North and South Army's which fostered Baseball's growth and popularity.

According to PBS, this was the official guide carried by the players for rules and regulations and there are less than ten known to exist.

The original publication binding was made from flexible cloth with a graphic imprinted in gold of a ballplayer and title.

It's extremely rare to find an original publication of "The Base Ball Player's Pocket Companion", let alone offered for purchase. If you do, it's most likely to be available via an auction. Past auction pricing has ranged from $4000 to over $39,000.

Though, "The Base Ball Player's Pocket Companion" in 1859 by Henry Chadwick is widely considered the first sole book published on Baseball, the "Manual of Cricket and Base Ball" (with Rules and Regulations illustrated) 24-page book published by Mayhew & Baker in 1958 covered the topic.

The chapter on "BASE BALL." Is covered on pages 20 through 24. I discovered a clean copy online from the

Boston Library and have included copies of the original published pages here.

Interesting to learn about the terms used in the mid-1800's to describe various elements of the game such as a pitcher was referred to as a "feeder" or "thrower". While a batter was called a "striker", a swing is "struck at", and at bats called "knocks".

There's many more fascinating terms and rules stating how the game was played on these pages and in "The Base Ball Player's Pocket Companion".

Here's the first page from the "Manual of Cricket and Base Ball." publication, then skipping to the chapter on "BASE BALL."

A MANUAL
of
CRICKET AND BASE BALL,
with
RULES AND REGULATIONS.
ILLUSTRATED.

THE CRICKET FIELD.

BOSTON:
MAYHEW & BAKER, 208 WASHINGTON ST.
1858.

Oxford shoes, or regular cricket shoes, with spiked-soles, complete the arrangement.

Sect. 6.—The Expenses.

24. Cricket may be played at very little expense, the price of balls, bats, and stumps being all that is really required; or it may be made a rather extravagant game, depending upon the outlay in non-essentials incident to matches, &c. The ground is the chief needful outlay, and sometimes that can be obtained all the year round for nothing, as in the neighborhood of common land. But here it cannot be preserved in tip-top order, and many irregularities will always exist. When, however, dinners are constantly being made up, and the expenses of going from home to matches are considered, it will be found that cricket, innocent as it is, may be made a source of considerable expense to a young man of limited income. To such, therefore, I would say, look well before you incur anything more than the club subscription, and you will thus often thereby avoid the payment of a bill five or six times as great as you had previously expected.

BASE BALL.

Base Ball now the favorite game throughout New England, besides an ordinary field, requires only a ball, and a bat, or stick resembling a common rolling pin but not quite so heavy, and of the same size all the way down. The Ball is the common one used in the games played with ball except cricket and football; and it is composed of a centre of cork or India rubber covered over with worsted, wound tightly in all directions so as to make a sphere, and finally covered with stout white sheep's skin, stiched in large sections.

The Game (*One out all out*) is played by first fixing four spots called " bases " at nearly equal distances, and marked by a stone or small plug. (See diagram.)

```
          C
          S
A                  D



      ( T )



B    40 feet.    C
```
(left side labeled 50 feet)

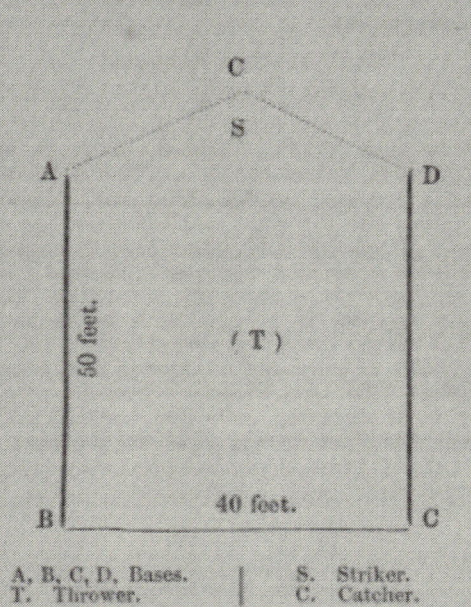

A, B, C, D, Bases.　　S. Striker.
T. Thrower.　　　　　C. Catcher.

In the centre of this is another place (T) called "the seat" where the "feeder" or thrower stands, to give or throw the ball to the one who has the bat, and who stands at (S) in the diagram. Two sides are chosen, one of which goes "in" while the other is "out;" this being decided by tossing up the bat, first marking it or by the rules annexed. There should not be less than ten or twelve players in all and twenty or thirty are not too many. The "in" side begin by standing at (S), in the diagram called "the house," one of them taking the bat, while the feeder who is one of the "out" party standing at his "seat," throws the ball at or in a line with his bat, after calling "play." The rest of the "out" party are distributed over the field round the outside of the bases (C), the catcher stands directly behind the striker at a distance of at least four feet to catch the ball and return it to the feeder. When the ball is thus given the batman's object is to hit it far and low over the field and his side put out at once. First, if he fails to strike after three trials, and the ball is caught each time by the "out" side; secondly, if he strikes it and it is caught by any of the "out" side before it falls to the ground or after a single hop or rebound, or thirdly if he is struck on the body after leaving his base and while not standing at another base. *The score* is made by the "in" party as follows:— Each player after striking the ball runs to the first base A, then to B, C and D, according to the distance he has knocked the ball, after passing D he calls "tally" and scores one, and if while running between the bases he is hit by the ball, his side is "out." After one of the "in" party has hit the ball and dropped the bat another takes his place; and on receiving the ball he strikes it or fails as the case may be. The object of the catcher and the balance of the "out" party is to catch the ball when struck or to hit the strikers while running between the several bases.

CLUB RULES FOR PLAYING BASE BALL.

1. In playing stated games of Base Ball a certain number of tallies shall be played for, (say 50,) the marking of which by either side shall constitute the game.
2. Sides shall be selected in this manner:—The President, or in his absence the Director, shall designate two members who may toss for the choice of players; and if more than one game is played the choosers shall be varied in each successive game.
3. Each player, as he is chosen, shall take his stand beside the player preceding him, in order that no confusion may ensue as to who or who has not been chosen; and every member intending to participate in the game shall endeavor to stand in full view of the choosers while the match is forming.
4. The game, unless a special agreement is made previous to commencing, shall be what is termed "one out all out."
5. The players choosing shall have absolute control of their respective sides during the game, (subject, however, to these rules,) and shall designate the place which each player shall occupy; and it shall be their duty to vary their thrower and catcher at least as often as at the close of every third

innings, in order to give those members who wish an opportunity to improve in throwing and catching.

6. If a sufficient number of members of the Club be not present at the time appointed for playing, persons not members may be chosen to make up the match, and the players so chosen shall retain their places until the game is played out; but in all cases members shall have the preference when present at the time of choosing.

7. If another player make his appearance on the ground after the game has commenced, (the sides being even,) the party having the choice shall not take him on his side until another player arrives to mate him, unless by permission of the chooser on the opposite side; but if there be a vacancy on either side he may be taken to fill such vacancy simply by notifying the opposite chooser.

8. Four bases or bounds shall constitute a round; the distance from first to second and from third to fourth base shall not be less than fifty feet, and from first to fourth and second to third not less than forty feet.

9. The striker shall stand inside of a space of four feet in diameter at equal distance between the first and fourth base; and the catcher shall not enter within those lines. The thrower shall stand at least thirty feet from the striker.

10. Players must take their knocks in the order in which they are chosen; and after the first innings is played the turn will commence with the player succeeding the one who lost on the previous innings.

11. The ball being struck at three times and missed, and caught each time by a player on the opposite side, the striker shall be considered out. Or if the ball be ticked or knocked and caught on the opposite side, the striker shall be considered out. But if the ball is not caught after being struck at three times it shall be considered a knock, and the striker obliged to run.

12. If a player while running the bounds be hit with the ball thrown by one of the opposite side, before he has touched the home goal, while off a base, he shall be considered out.

13. A player shall not be considered on a base unless he is within a foot of it. And any player struck by the ball at more than that distance is out.

14. When playing "each one for himself," or "one out—one out," twice catch behind shall be considered out; three times knock to be allowed, and the same rules to be observed as in "one out all out," with this exception, viz: the

match shall consist of a certain number of innings on each side, as may be agreed upon by the choosers, and the side marking the highest number of tallies at the close of their respective innings shall be judged the winner.

15. A player having possession of the first base when the ball is struck by the succeeding player, must vacate the base, even at the risk of being put out; and when two players get on one base, either by accident or otherwise, the player who arrives last is entitled to the base.

16. The ball being caught on the first bound from the ground shall be considered fair in all instances.

17. When no judges or referees are appointed, and a dispute arise, the two members choosing shall act as umpires in the matter; and in case they fail to settle the dispute they shall select one of the bystanders to whom the matter in question shall be referred—and his decision shall be final and binding upon all parties.

18. No member, engaged on either side, shall withdraw during the progress of the game, without first notifying the chooser of his intention.

19. These Rules shall not be altered or amended except by a vote of two-thirds of the members present at a regularly called meeting; but all, or any portion of them, may be suspended during any one game by a vote of the majority of members present at the time of choosing sides.

Since the physical book, "The Base Ball Player's Pocket Companion" in 1859 by Mayhew & Baker, is such a rare find and considered by historians and collectors the most important early Baseball book, I decided it would be a valuable addition to any home library who love the game.

Thus, Baseball Classics has published this public domain literature so avid Baseball fans can add it to their library.

Rather than copy and paste images of the text from the internet, it has been re-produced based on the original. This includes the exact content, original illustrations, any typos, grammatical errors, blank pages, and page numbering.

Enjoy this important, historic literature from the earliest publication on America's national pastime!

Dean Patino
Baseball Classics Founder

The Base Ball Player's Pocket Companion
Table of Contents

"New York Game" Diagram of Base Ball Field	2
The Base Ball Player's Pocket Companion	3
Officers of the Massachusetts Association of Base Ball	4
The Massachusetts Game Of Base Ball	5
Constitution	12
By-Laws	16
Rules and Regulations	20
The New York Game Of Base Ball	25
Rules and Regulations (National Association of Base Ball Players)	27

"New York Game."

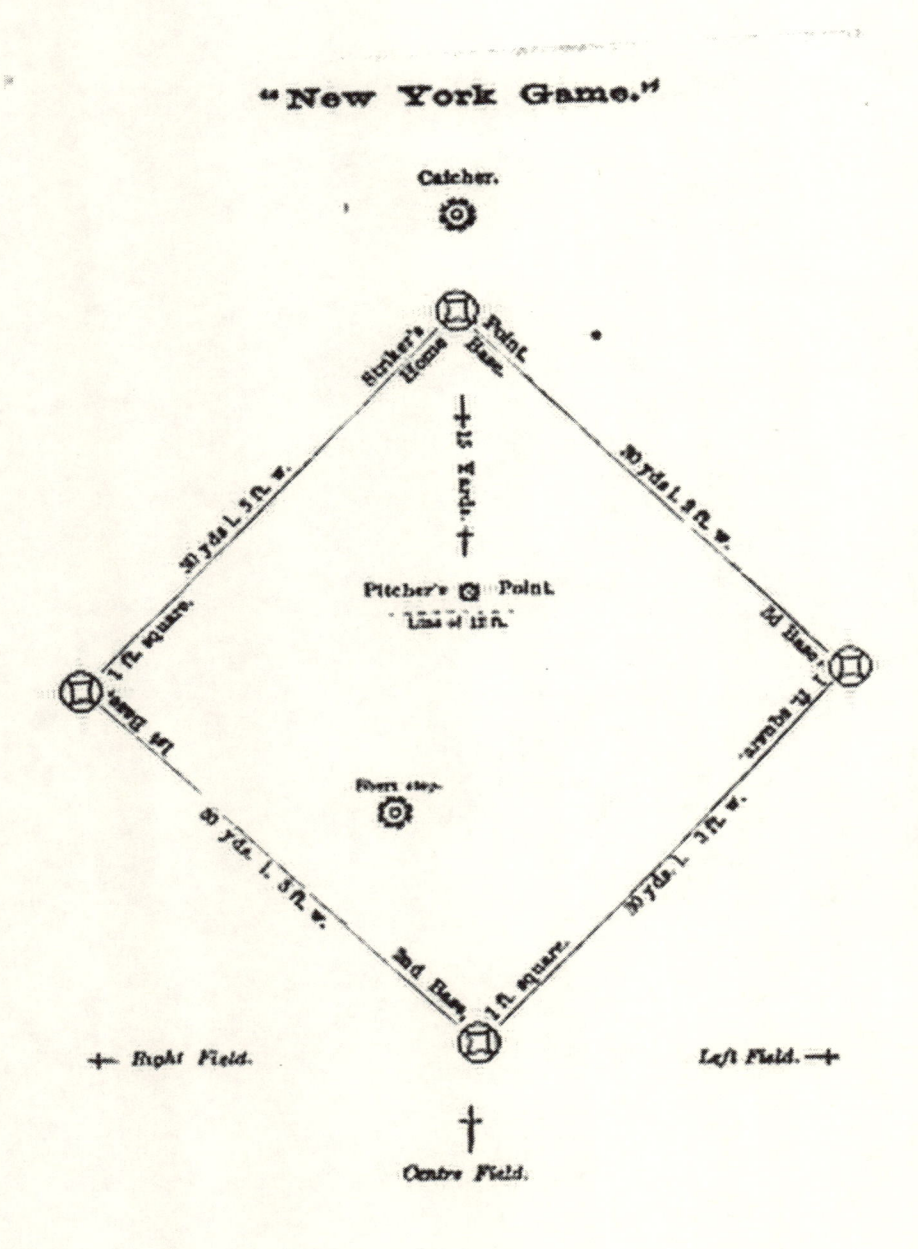

Catcher.

Striker's Point — Home Base.

45 ft.

Pitcher's Point.
Lines at 12 ft.

30 yds. 1 ft. w.

30 yds. 1 ft. w.

1st Base — 1 ft. square.

3d Base — 1 ft. square.

30 yds. 1 ft. w.

30 yds. 1 ft. w.

Short stop.

2nd Base — 1 ft. square.

← Right Field.   Left Field. →

Centre Field.

Diagram of Base Ball Field.

THE

Base Ball Player's

𝔓𝔬𝔠𝔨𝔢𝔱 ℭ𝔬𝔪𝔭𝔞𝔫𝔦𝔬𝔫 :

CONTAINING

Rules and Regulations for Forming Clubs,

DIRECTIONS FOR PLAYING THE

"MASSACHUSETTS GAME"

AND THE

"NEW YORK GAME,"
FROM OFFICIAL REPORTS.

———

ILLUSTRATED, CLOTH

———

BOSTON;
MAYHEW & BAKER, 208 WASHINGTON STREET,
1859.

OFFICERS OF THE
Massachusetts Association of Base Ball Players
FOR 1859.

President,
P. R. JOHNSON, of WINTEROP CLUB, Holliston.
Vice President,
E. E. NELSON, of EXCELSIOR CLUB, Upton.
Secretary,
A. S. FLYE, of OLYMPIC CLUB, Boston.
Treasurer,
A. S. HARDING, of UNION CLUB, Medway.

Names of Clubs belonging to the Association. 1859.

ALPHA CLUB, Ashland.
AMERICAN CLUB, South Dedham.
ANNAWAN CLUB, Mansfield.
BAY STATE CLUB, Boston.
BUNKER EEL CLUB, Charlestown.
EAGLE CLUB, Westboro'.
EXCELSIOR CLUB, Upton.
FORREST CLUB, East Cambridge.
MASSAPOAG CLUB, Sharon.
MECHANICS CLUB, Waltham.
NEPONSET CLUB, Walpole Centre.
OLENPIC CLUB, Boston.
ROUGH AND READY CLUB, S. Walpole.
SOUTH SHORE CLUB, No. Weymouth.
UNION CLUB, Medway.
WADAQUODOCK CLUB, Bolton
WARREN CLUB, Roxbury.
WINTHROP CLUB, Holliston.
WOPOWAGE CLUB, Milford
YANKEE CLUB, Natick.

THE MASSACHUSETTS GAME
OF
BASE BALL.

The Game of Base Ball, as adopted by the "Massachusetts Association of Base Ball Players," May 1858, which has ever been the favorite and principal game played throughout New England, differs, in many points, from the New York game, though it requires equal skill and activity, and deservedly holds the first place in the estimation of all ball players and the public.

It is only within the last four years that match games have become popular, and that this game of base ball has taken the high position which it now occupies, as the leading game of out-door sports. The popularity of, and the increasing interest in, this game, is mainly to be attributed to the public journals, which have supported and encouraged its participants, by reporting their matches, and advocating their claims to public favor, as important and necessary as a branch of physical education.

The only essential materials used in playing the game, besides a ball, are a bat-stick and four wooden stakes for bases, the form and sizes of which are described in the annexed rules and regulations of the game. The ball is composed of woollen yarn and strips of India rubber wound tightly, forming a complete sphere, and covered with buck or calf skin.

The game is commenced by staking off a square of 60 feet for the bases, and measuring the distance of 30 feet from the thrower's to the striker's stand, as explained by the following diagram:

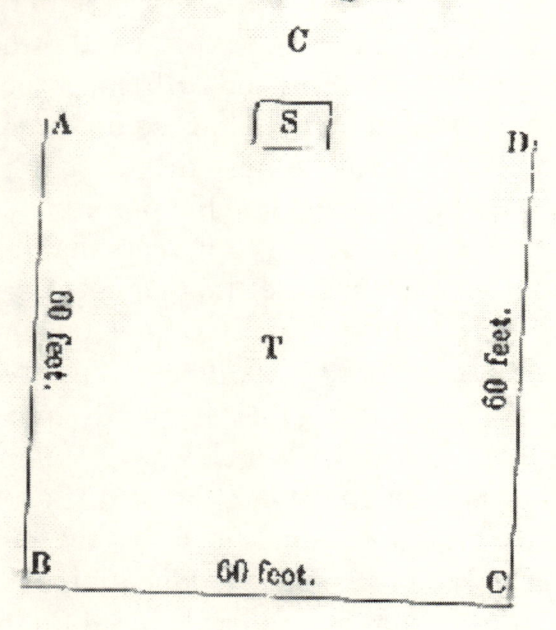

```
              C
    A       ┌─┐        D
            │S│
            └─┘

    │                    │
 60 feet.      T      60 feet.
    │                    │

    B ────── 60 feet. ────── C
```

The four corners of the square (A, B, C, and D,) are the bases. The square (S,) of four feet, at equal distance between the first and fourth base (A and D,)

OF BASE BALL.

is the striker's stand. Outside of this square and the line between the first and fourth base, is the catcher's stand. In the centre of the square (T,) the thrower is stationed, who delivers the ball to the striker, which, if not struck. Which, if not struck, should be caught by the catcher behind; but if struck by the batsman, he is obliged to run the bases, commencing by the batsman, he is obliged to run the bases, commencing at A, so on to B, C, and D; when arriving at D; or the home base, he is entitled to one tally. After the first player strikes the ball and runs to the base, he is immediately succeeded by the next "in" player, who takes his turn in the order in which he is chosen. The "out" party, besides the thrower and catcher, should be stationed as follows: One player on or within a few feet from each base, who should give strict attention to the game, and be prepared to receive the ball at any time, in order to "put out" an opposite player, while passing from one base to the other. One or two players should be stationed a few yards behind the catcher, to stop the ball in case the catcher should fail to do so. The other players should be stationed at different parts of the field, to pass the ball to the thrower when it has been knocked by the striker.

The Rules and Regulations contained in this book, govern all match games, and are the only standard in the New England States.

The Olympic Club, of Boston, established in 1854, was the first regularly organized Club in the State, and for over a year the only one in the field. Its first match game was in the summer of 1855, with the Elm Tree Club. The "Elm Trees" only existed for a short time, many of its *branches* taking part in the formation of other Clubs. In 1856, the Green Mountain was established in Boston, and, during the season, several exciting match games were played on the Common, between them and the Olympics. During the season of 1857, many Clubs were organized in the vicinity of Boston, among which were the Bay State, Tri-Mountain, Bunker Hill, American, Rough and Ready, Massapong, Union, and Winthrop. A large number of matches were played, and a great degree of interest manifested among Ball players and in course of the season, the Olympics famed a code of Rules and Regulations which was adopted by several of Clubs. At the opening of the season of 1858, there was a general movement in favor of calling a convention of delegates from the several Clubs, for the purpose of establishing a code of regulations to govern all matches between them; and according to a call signed by the Presidents of six of the senior Clubs, a Convention was held in Dedham, May 13, 1858, at which ten Clubs were represented by two delegates each. A resolution was adopted declaring the Convention a permanent organization, and a committee of five was appointed to prepare and submit a Constitution and By-Laws for its government;

OF BASE BALL.

THE THROWER.

also, Rules and Regulations for playing Base Ball. The committee reported, and the Convention adopted the Constitution and By-Laws, and was duly organized under the name of the "MASSACHUSETTS ASSOCIATION OF BASE BALL PLAYERS." The Rules and Regulations of the game were then adopted by the Association, and the Chairman of the Committee was appointed to superintendent the publishing of the same.

CONSTITUTION.

This Association shall be known by the name of the "MASSACHUSETTS ASSOCIATION OF BASE BALL PLAYERS."

ARTICLE I.

The object of the Association shall be to improve and foster the Massachusetts game of Base Ball, and the cultivation of kindly feelings among the different members of Base Ball Clubs in this State.

ARTICLE II. – *Members.*

SEC. 1. The Association shall be composed of two delegates from each of the Base Ball Clubs in this State which have been duly admitted to a representation in the Convention forming this Constitution.

SEC. 2. Any Base Ball Club, desiring to be represented in this Association, shall present to the Secretary, at least two weeks before the annual meeting of the Association, a written application, signed by its President and Secretary, setting forth the name of the Club, its officers and delegates, and such Club shall be declared duly entitled to representation in this Association by paying to the Treasurer the sum of one dollar.

Sec. 3. No Club shall be represented in this Association until its delegates have signed this Constitution.

ARTICLE III. – *Officers.*

Sec. 1. The officers of this Association shall be a President, Vice President, Secretary and Treasurer.

Sec. 2. The first election of officers shall be held immediately upon the adoption of this Constitution, and the officers then elected shall respectively hold office until the next annual meeting, and thereafter all officers shall be elected by written ballot and general ticket, a plurality of votes electing.

Sec. 3. Each officer shall hold his office of appointment for one year.

Sec. 4. Any vacancy in either of the offices may be filled at any meeting of the Association regularly organized.

ARTICLE IV. – *Duties of Officers.*

Sec. 1. It shall be the duty of the President to preside at all meetings of the Association, to preserve order, and see that the laws are carried into effect. He shall have no vote, except in the election of officers, and except in cases of an equal division of the members on any question, when he shall give the casting vote.

Sec. 2. The President shall have power to call special meetings of the Association whenever he may deem it expedient, and he shall authorize the Secretary to call a special meeting whenever requested to do so, in writing, by five Clubs. He shall appoint all Committees unless otherwise ordered.

Sec. 3. The Vice President, in the absence of the President, shall be invested with the power of that office, and perform all the duties of the office.

Sec. 4. The Secretary shall be a medium of communication with other Associations, and the public. He shall retain copies of all letters received by him. He shall affix his name to all advertisements and notices of the Association, unless otherwise ordered. He shall attend all meetings of the Association, and, I the absence of the President and Vice President, he shall call the same to order. He shall accurately record the proceedings of all meetings in the journal of the Association, also notify Clubs of their election, and issue all notices of meetings. He shall deliver to his successor in office, all books or other property belonging to the Association, in his procession.

Sec. 5. The Treasurer shall receive and hold all the funds of the Association. He shall keep a correct account of all money received and disbursed by him, in a book to be provided for that purpose. He shall pay no bills unless approved by the President or a majority of members; he shall have power to assess each Club their proportionate part of any sum paid out by him, when authorized to do so by a vote of the Association. He shall be prepared to report the amount of funds in his possession at the annual meeting, and whenever requested by a vote of the Association.

ARTICLE V. – *Meetings.*

SEC. 1. The annual meeting of the Association shall be held on the first Saturday in April, at such hour and place in the city of Boston as the President shall select.

SEC. 2. All meetings of the Association shall be advertised in one or more of the daily journals of the city of Boston, at least one week previous to that of the meeting; and, when a special meeting is called, its nature shall be stated in the announcement of the meeting.

SEC. 3. At all meetings of the Association, fifteen delegates shall constitute a quorum for the transaction of business.

ARTICLE VI. – *Rules.*

The Rules and Regulations herewith annexed shall govern all match games of Base Ball played between Clubs belonging to this Association.

ARTICLE VII. – *Amendments.*

No alterations, additions or amendments to the Constitution and By-Laws, or the Rules and Regulations, shall be adopted, unless the same shall be submitted to the annual meeting, nor unless the name shall be adopted by a vote of a majority of all the members present at such meeting.

BY-LAWS.

SEC. 1. The order of business at all meetings shall be as follows: – 1st. Reading the Report of Previous Meetings. 2d. Election of Officers. 3d. Report of Committees in order of their appointment. 4th. Report of Officers. 5th. Unfinished business. 6th. New business.

SEC. 2. No member shall be allowed to discuss any question under debate without rising and addressing the Chair; nor shall be speak more than twice on any question, nor more than five minutes at any time, unless by unanimous consent.

SEC. 3. Every member present, shall be required to

OF BASE BALL. 17

THE STRIKER.

THE MASSACHUSETTS GAME OF BASE BALL.

vote on questions, unless he is directly or personally interested, or excused by the vote of a majority of members present.

SEC. 4. Any member may at any time call for the reading of any article of the Constitution or By-Laws, or minutes, or any other paper relating to the question then under consideration.

SEC. 5. The yeas and nays shall be taken on any question, at the request of five members.

SEC. 6. Any member belonging to this Association, behaving in an ungentlemanly manner, or rendering himself obnoxious to the Association, may, by a vote of two-thirds of the members present, be expelled.

SEC. 7. All charges against any member or Club must be submitted in writing, and notice of such charges furnished such members or Clubs so charged, who shall be entitled to submit a written defence.

THE MASSACHUSETTS GAME.

RULES AND REGULATIONS

Of the Game of Base Ball, adopted by the "Massachusetts Association of Base Ball Players," held in Dedham, May 13th, 1858.

1. The BALL must weigh not less than two, nor more than two and three-quarter ounces, avoirdupois. It must measure not less than six and a half inches in circumference, and must be covered with leather.
2. The BAT must be round, and must not exceed two and a half inches in diameter in the thickest part. It must be made of wood, and may be of any length to suit the Striker.
3. Four BASES or BOUNDS shall constitute a round; the distance from each Base shall be sixty feet.
4. The BASES shall be wooden stakes, projecting four feet from the ground.
5. The STRIKER shall stand inside of a space of four feet in diameter, at equal distance between the first and fourth Bases.
6. The BALL must weigh not less than two, nor more than two and three-quarter ounces, avoirdupois. It must measure not less than six and a half inches in circumference, and must be covered with leather.
7. The CATCHER shall not enter within the space occupied by the Striker, and must remain upon his feet in all cases while catching the Ball.

OF BASE BALL.

8. The Ball must be thrown–not pitched or tossed–to the Bat, on the side preferred by the Striker, and within reach of his Bat.
9. The Ball must be caught flying in all cases.
10. Players must take their knocks in the order in which they are numbered; and after the first innings is played, the turn will commence with the player succeeding the one who lost on the previous innings.
11. The Ball being stuck at three times and missed, and caught each time by a player on the opposite side, the Striker shall be considered out. Or, if the Ball be ticked or knocked, and caught out. But if the Ball is not caught after being stuck at three times, it shall be considered a knock, and the Striker obliged to run.
12. Should the Striker stand at the Bat without striking at good balls thrown repeatedly at him, for the apparent purpose of delaying the game, or of giving advantage to players, the referees, after warning him, shall call *one strike*, and if he persists in such action, *two* and *three strikes*; when three strikes are called, he shall be subject to the same rules as if he stuck at three fair balls.
13. A player, having possession of the first Base, when the Ball is struck by the succeeding player, must vacate the Base, even at the risk of being put out; and when two players get on one Base, either by

accident or otherwise, the player who arrived last is entitled to the Base.

14. If a player, while running the Bases, be hit with the Ball thrown by one of the opposite side, before he has touched the home bound, while off a Base, he shall be considered out.
15. A player, after running the four Bases, on making the home bound, shall be entitled to one tally.
16. In playing all match games, when one is out, the side shall be considered out.
17. In playing all match games, one hundred tallies shall constitute the game, the making of which be either Club, shall constitute a match in all games.
18. Not less than ten nor more than fourteen players from each Club, shall constitute a match in all games.
19. A person engaged on either side, shall not withdraw during the progress of the match, unless he be disabled, or by the consent of the opposite party.
20. The referee shall be chosen as follows:– One from each Club, who shall agree upon a third man from some Club belonging to this Association, if possible. Their decision shall be final, and binding upon both parties.
21. The Tallymen shall be chosen in the same manner as the Referees.

THE CATCHER.

THE NEW YORK GAME
OF
BASE BALL.

The Game of Base Ball is fast becoming, in this country, what Cricket is to England, a national game, combining, as it does, exciting sport and healthful exercise at a trifling expense. It has a decided advantage over the monotonous routine of the Gymnasium or other modes of exercise.

The rules adopted by the National Association of Base Ball Players, who meet annually in New York, are rapidly being adopted by players in all parts of the country, they having been found superior to all others as giving a more equal share in the game to all the players engaged, as the game, when properly played, requires close attention, courage and activity; and the victory in a match depends as much upon the excellence of the fielding as on that of the players in more prominent positions. The first Club formed in New England, under these rules, was organized June 16th, 1857, under the name of the "Tri-Mountain Base Ball Club of Boston," and for a long period was the only one in this section of the country. Like all new ideas not thoroughly understood, this innovation upon the "old style" of play met with decided and marked opposition, and it was only with the most determined pluck and perseverance that the founders kept the club together, and sustained the claims of the game adopted by the National Association as superior to all others. But, in the Spring and Summer of 1858, many new clubs formed, among which were the Portland and Forrest City Clubs, of Portland, Me.; the Pioneer, of Springfield, Mass.; the Atwater, of Westfield; the Nonotuck, Union and Excelsior of Northhampton, the Lawrence and Independent, of Cambridge; and in the Spring of 1859, the Bowdoin, of Boston. An exciting match played in Boston in the Summer of 1858 between the Portland Club and the Tri-Mountain, did much to remove the prejudices of many of the opponents of the game, and produced a marked change of opinion in its favor; it may now be considered as firmly established in New England, and we trust the day is not far distant when the rules of the National Association will govern all matches played in the country.

RULES AND REGULATIONS
OF
THE GAME OF BASE BALL,

ADOPTED BY THE

National Association of Base Ball Players,

HELD IN NEW-YORK, MARCH 19, 1859.

SEC. 1. The ball must weigh not less than five and three-fourths nor more than six ounces avoirdupois. It must measure not less than nine and three-fourths, nor more than ten inches in circumference. It must be composed of India rubber and yarn, and covered with leather, and in all match games shall be furnished by the challenging Club, and become property of the winning Club, as a trophy of victory.

SEC. 2. The bat must be round, and must not exceed two and half inches in diameter in the thickest part. It must be made of wood, and may be of any length to suit the striker.

SEC. 3. The bases must be four in number, placed at equal distances from each other, and securely fastened upon the four corners of a square, whose sides are respectively thirty yards. The must be so constructed as to be distinctly seen by the umpire, and must cover a space equal to one square foot of surface. The first, second and third bases shall be canvass bags painted white, and filled with sand or saw-dust; the home base and pitcher's point to be each marked by a flat circular iron plate, painted or enamelled white.

Sec. 4. The base from which the ball is struck shall be designated the Home Base, and must be directly opposite to the second base; the first base must always be that upon the right hand, and the third base that upon the left hand side of the striker, when occupying his position at the home base.

Sec. 5. The pitcher's position shall be designated by a line four yards in length, drawn at right angles to a line from home to the second base, having its centre upon that line, at a fixed iron plate placed at a point fifteen yards distant from the home base. The pitcher must deliver the ball as near as possible over the centre of said base, and for the striker.

Sec. 6. The ball must be pitched, not jerked nor thrown to the bat; and whenever the pitcher draws back his hand, or moves with the apparent purpose or pretension to deliver the ball, he shall so deliver it, and must have neither foot in advance of the line at the time of delivering the ball; and if he fails in either of these particulars, then it shall be declared a baulk.

RULES AND REGULATIONS.   29

SEC. 7. When a. baulk is made by the pitcher, every player running the bases is entitled to one base, without being put out.

SEC. 8. If the ball, from a stroke of the bat, is caught behind the range of home and the first base or home and the third base, without having touched the ground, or first touches the ground behind those bases, it shall be termed foul, and must be so declared by the umpire unasked. If the ball first touches the ground, or is caught without having touched the ground, either upon or in front of the range of those bases, it shall be considered fair.

SEC. 9. A player making the home base, shall be entitled to score one run.

SEC. 10. If three balls are stuck at and missed, and the last one is not caught, either flying or upon the first bound, it shall be considered fair, and the striker must attempt to make his run.

SEC. 11. The striker is out if a foul ball is caught, either before touching the ground, or upon the first bound;

SEC. 12. Or, if three balls are struck at and missed, and the last is caught either before touching the ground, or upon the first bound;

SEC. 13. Or, if a fair ball is struck, and the ball is caught either without having touched the ground or upon the first bound;

Sec. 14. Or, if a fair ball is struck, and the ball is held by an adversary on the first base, before the striker touches that base;

Sec. 15. Of if, at any time, he is touched by the ball while in play in the hands of an adversary, without some part of his person being on a base.

Sec. 16. No ace nor base can be made upon a foul ball, nor when a fair ball has been caught without having touched the ground, and the ball shall, in the former instance, be considered dead, and not in play until it shall first have been settled in the hands of the pitcher; in either case, the players running bases shall return to them.

Sec. 17. The striker must stand on a line drawn through the centre of the home base, not exceeding in length three feet from either side thereof, and parallel with the line occupied by the pitcher. He shall be considered the striker until he has made the first base. Players must strike in regular rotation, and after the first inning is played, the turn commences with the player who stands on the list next to the one who lost the third hand.

Sec. 18. Players must make their bases in the order of striking; and when a fair ball is struck, and not caught nor on the first bound, the first base must be vacated, as also the second and third bases, if they are occupied at the same time. Players may be

31

BASE TENDER.

RULES AND REGULATIONS. 33

put out upon any base, under these circumstances, in the same manner as the striker, when running to the first base.

SEC. 19. Players running the bases must, so far as possible, keep upon the direct line between the bases; and should any player run three feet out of this line, for the purpose of avoiding the ball in the hands of the adversary, he shall be declared out.

SEC. 20. Any player, who shall intentionally prevent an adversary from catching or fielding the ball, shall be declared out.

SEC. 21. If a player is prevented from making a base, by the intentional obstruction of an adversary, he shall be entitled to that base, and not be put out.

SEC. 22. If an adversary stops the ball with his hat or cap, or takes it from the hands of a party not engaged in the game, no player can be put out unless the ball shall first have been settled in the hands of the pitcher.

SEC. 23. If a ball, from the stroke of the bat, is held under any other circumstances than as enumerated in Section 22nd, and without having touched the ground more than once, the striker is out.

SEC. 24. If two hands are already out, no player running home at the time a ball is struck, can make an ace if the striker is put out.

RULES AND REGULATIONS.

Sec. 25. An innings must be concluded at the time the third hand is put out.

Sec. 26. The game shall consist of nine innings to each side, when, should the number of runs be equal, the play shall be continued until a majority of runs, upon an equal number of innings shall be declared, which shall conclude the game.

Sec. 27. If playing all matches, nine players from each club shall constitute a full field, and they must have been regular members of the club which they represent, and of no other club, for thirty days prior to the match. No change or substitution shall be made after the game has been commenced, unless for reason of illness or injury. Position of players and choice of innings shall be determined by captains, previously appointed for that purpose by the respective clubs.

Sec. 28. The umpire shall take care that the regulations respecting the ball, bats, bases and the pitcher's and striker's position are strictly observed. He shall keep a record of the game in a book prepared for the purpose; he shall be the judge of fair and unfair play, and shall determine all disputes and differences which may occur during the game; he shall take especial care to declare all foul balls and baulks immediately upon their occurrence, unasked, and in a distinct and audible manner.

RULES AND REGULATIONS. 35

Sec. 29. In all matches, the umpire shall be selected by the captains of the respective sides, and shall perform all the duties enumerated in Section 28, except recording the game, which shall be done by two scorers, one of whom shall be appointed by each of the contending clubs.

Sec. 30. No person engaged in a match, either as umpire, scorer or player, shall be either directly or indirectly interested in any bet upon the game. Neither umpire, scorer or player shall be changed during a match, unless with the consent of both parties, except for a violation of this law, and except as provided in Section 27, and then the umpire may dismiss any transgressor.

Sec. 31. The umpire in any match shall determine when play shall be suspended; and if the game cannot be concluded, it shall be decided by the last even innings, provided five innings have been played, and the party having the greatest number of runs shall be declared the winner.

Sec. 32. Clubs may adopt such rules respecting balls knocked beyond or outside the bounds of the field, as the circumstances of the ground may demand, and these rules shall govern all matches played upon the ground, provided that they are distinctly made known to every player and umpire previous to the commencement of the game.

(For Plan of Laying out the grounds for this Game, see Diagram, Frontispiece.)

Uniform with Base Ball Player's Companion.

THE

CRICKET PLAYER'S

POCKET COMPANION.

CONTAINING

Plans for Laying Out the Grounds,

FORMING CLUBS, &c., &c.,

TO WHICH ARE ADDED

RULES AND REGULATIONS FOR CRICKET,

ADOPTED BY THE

MARY-LE-BONE CLUB.

BOSTON;
MAYHEW & BAKER, 208 WASHINGTON STREET,
1859.

Afterword

Suffice to say, the Massachusetts Association of Base Ball Players and the National Association of Base Ball Players held in New York, played a significant role ultimately towards the formation of Major League Baseball.

Baseball in the 1700s

Baseball, as a structured sport, evolved from older bat-and-ball games such as rounders and cricket in England. During the 1700s, these games were played by children and adults alike, but they did not resemble the organized sport of baseball today. Instead, they were more informal games that varied greatly in their rules and equipment from one locality to another.

One of the earliest forms of these games was "stoolball," referenced as far back as the 14th century and played in England. Stoolball involved pitching a ball to a batter who defended a target, which was often a stool. This game is sometimes cited as a precursor to both cricket and baseball. By the 18th century, cricket was well established and gaining popularity in England, particularly among the upper classes, while rounders was more associated with children and the lower classes.

Rounders, which shared more similarities with baseball than cricket did, typically involved hitting a small, hard ball with a rounded bat and running around a circuit of bases to score. The rules were not standardized, and the game was often played in meadows, streets, or village greens, with rudimentary equipment.

The evolution of these bat-and-ball games from the 1700s into modern baseball is a complex process that unfolded over the next century, particularly in North America. The game of "town ball" or "base" became popular in the United States, which was a local variation of rounders. It is these American versions of bat-and-ball games that directly contributed to what would become known as baseball.

By the late 1700s and early 1800s, these games were being played in North America by colonists and Native Americans alike. There are references to a game called "baseball" being played in North America in the 18th century, but the descriptions of the game's play and rules suggest that it was likely a version of rounders or similar to town ball.

It was not until the mid-19th century that baseball began to take its modern form with the establishment of the Knickerbocker Base Ball Club in New York City in 1845. The club is credited with codifying a set of rules for baseball that laid the foundation for the organized sport, including the use of a diamond-shaped infield and three-strike rule.

In summary, while the 1700s saw the play of various bat-and-ball games that can be considered ancestors to baseball, the version of the sport we are familiar with today did not exist at that time. It was these early games that set the stage for the development of baseball in the 19th century, which would grow to become America's beloved pastime.

Studying the origins of baseball in the 1700s is an exploration of the cultural and recreational life of the era. It shows how games evolve to fit the societies in which they are played and how they can be a barometer of social change. For the avid baseball fan, understanding the historical context of these games provides a deeper appreciation for the sport and its special place in the history of recreation and competition.

The 1700s contributed to the fabric of baseball's history not through structured leagues or iconic players, but through the slow development of a pastime that would come to capture the imagination and passion of future generations. It was a period where the seeds were sown for a sport that would become intricately woven into the cultural tapestry of nations, particularly the United States. Baseball's journey from the informal games of the 1700s to the well-defined sport of the 19th and 20th centuries is a testament to the game's enduring appeal and its ability to adapt and resonate with successive generations of players and fans alike.

Baseball in the 1800s

Baseball in the 1800s saw its transformation from a recreational pastime to a professional sport, reflecting broader changes in American society. The century began with various regional games resembling baseball, the most prominent being rounders in England and town ball in the United States. By the 1840s, the game we recognize as baseball was emerging in the New York area, where in 1845, the New York Knickerbocker Baseball Club codified a set of rules, which notably included three-strikes rules and the elimination of "soaking" or "plugging" the runner (hitting the runner with the thrown ball to get him out).

The Civil War era played a significant role in spreading the game. Soldiers from New York introduced their fellow servicemen to the New York version of baseball, and these men took the game back home with them after the war. By the late 1860s, baseball was rapidly becoming America's national pastime.

Professionalism started to take root in the latter half of the 19th century. The first openly all-professional baseball team, the Cincinnati Red Stockings, was established in 1869, embarking on a nationwide tour and going undefeated. Their success led to the formation of the National Association of Professional Base Ball Players in 1871, considered by some historians to be the first major league.

Baseball's rules and equipment evolved significantly during this period. Overhand pitching was introduced, distances between bases and the pitcher's mound were standardized, and the invention of the catcher's mitt, along with other protective equipment, changed how the game was played.

However, the 1800s also bore witness to the game's darker side, with issues such as gambling, cheating, and exclusions based on race. Despite the creation of the color line barring African American players from the professional leagues, baseball continued to grow in popularity, with the formation of the National League in 1876 and the American Association in 1882, setting the stage for the modern World Series that would begin in the 20th century.

The end of the century saw stars like Cap Anson, Cy Young, and Honus Wagner, whose legacies would be celebrated for generations to come. Meanwhile, off the field, baseball's business side became increasingly sophisticated, with team owners seeking new ways to monetize the game, including the development of ballpark concessions and advertising.

The 19th century laid the foundational stones of baseball, setting up the structures, cultures, and controversies that would shape the sport for the next hundred years and beyond. Owning books like "The Base Ball Player's Pocket Companion" offers fans a direct connection to the early days of the sport, allowing them to understand the roots of modern baseball, appreciate its evolution, and gain insights into how the game's original strategies and rules have influenced the way it is played today.

The National League of Professional Baseball Clubs
The National League of Professional Baseball Clubs, commonly known as the National League (NL), is the older of the two leagues constituting Major League Baseball (MLB) in the United States and Canada, and the world's oldest current professional team sports league. Officially founded on February 2, 1876, by Chicago White Stockings' owner William Hulbert, the NL effectively replaced the National Association of Professional Base Ball Players (NAPBBP), which had been plagued by instability and disorder.

Hulbert, who became the league's first president, was a baseball visionary who saw the need for a more structured and disciplined organization that could provide more reliable schedules, standardized playing rules, and integrity both on and off the field. The impetus for forming the National League was to combat the rampant professionalism that had taken hold in the game, which was threatening its survival.

The establishment of the National League marked a significant turning point in the history of baseball. It introduced several key innovations that have shaped the sport ever since:

Exclusive Territories: The National League established exclusive territories for its member clubs, effectively barring other professional teams from entering their cities.

Revenues: It centralized control over the teams' schedules and gate receipts, helping to stabilize team revenues.

Player Contracts: The league introduced the "reserve clause," which bound players to their teams indefinitely, a precursor to the modern system of player contracts.

Game Rules: It began the process of standardizing the rules and equipment of baseball, which was necessary for a more uniform competition.

Integrity: Perhaps most critically, the National League sought to curb gambling and drinking, both by players and spectators, to clean up baseball's image.

The original league consisted of eight teams:
- Boston Red Stockings (now the Atlanta Braves),
- Chicago White Stockings (now the Chicago Cubs),
- Cincinnati Red Stockings (which disbanded in 1880)
- Hartford Dark Blues
- Louisville Grays
- New York Mutuals
- Philadelphia Athletics
- St. Louis Brown Stockings

The National League's early years were not without struggle. Teams faced financial difficulties, and competition from other leagues, particularly the American Association, posed significant challenges. However, the NL survived these battles, largely due to its strong leadership and commitment to the integrity of the game.

By the end of the 19th century, the National League had established itself as the premier baseball league in the United States. The NL's success eventually led to the creation of the American League, which was established as a second major league in 1901, and with which the NL negotiated a National Agreement to govern the sport. This partnership laid the foundation for the World Series, which began in 1903, formalizing the competition between the champions of the two leagues and solidifying baseball's place as America's national pastime.

Over the decades, the National League has seen some of baseball's greatest teams and players. It has been home to legends such as Cy Young, Honus Wagner, Christy Mathewson, and later stars like Willie Mays, Hank Aaron, and Sandy Koufax. The league's history is a rich tapestry of pioneering moments, dramatic pennant races, and iconic World Series matchups.

The formation of the National League represented a critical juncture in the evolution of professional baseball. It established the framework for today's game, embodying principles that would lead to the sport's growth and stability. For fans and historians alike, the National League's creation is a cornerstone event that underscores the organizational, cultural, and competitive facets of baseball. Its impact can still be felt in the modern era, making its formation a key chapter in the annals of the sport.

The American Association of Professional Baseball Clubs
The American Association (AA) was a professional baseball league that challenged the National League's (NL) dominance and brought about significant changes to the sport. Established in 1881, the AA began play in 1882 and was sometimes called "The Beer and Whiskey League" because it was backed by brewers and distillers

and because it allowed the sale of alcohol at its games, unlike the NL.

The AA was conceived by visionary businessmen who saw an opportunity to capitalize on the popularity of baseball by offering an alternative to the NL, which was criticized for its high-ticket prices and for forbidding games on Sunday, the only day off for most workers at that time. The AA aimed to appeal to the working-class demographic by addressing these two issues—lowering ticket prices to 25 cents (half of what the NL charged) and scheduling games on Sundays.

The original founders of the AA were owners of teams in Cincinnati, Louisville, St. Louis, and Philadelphia, cities that were either expelled from or felt poorly served by the NL. These owners were joined by others from Pittsburgh, Baltimore, and New York to form an eight-team league. The AA positioned itself as more populist and player friendly. It abolished the NL's reserve clause, which bound players to one team indefinitely, allowing for more player movement and better salaries.

The AA's existence led to a competitive environment between the two leagues. This competition played out not only in the pursuit of fan attendance but also in the battle for player talent. The rivalry escalated into a bidding war for players, which benefited the players but often strained the finances of the teams.

The AA saw several successful franchises, such as the St. Louis Browns (now the Cardinals) and the Cincinnati Red Stockings, and it contributed to the development of many baseball staples. It introduced the idea of a "minor league" farm system and pioneered the concept of revenue sharing from ticket sales, which are still fundamental to professional sports today.

However, the league faced numerous challenges. Financial instability was common among teams, and the quality of play was sometimes viewed as inferior to the NL. Despite a strong start, the AA struggled to maintain profitable franchises, leading to teams either folding or jumping to the NL.

The AA and NL occasionally attempted to find common ground, which led to the creation of an interleague championship that eventually evolved into the modern World Series. However, these agreements were often fraught with disputes, and the leagues continued to vie for dominance.

The AA's most significant impact may have been its role in the eventual merger with the NL in 1891. After the 1891 season, four AA teams were absorbed into the NL: the St. Louis Browns, Louisville Colonels, Washington Senators, and Baltimore Orioles. This merger effectively ended the AA and brought about a single "big league" that was a precursor to the modern Major League Baseball.

In retrospect, the American Association played a crucial role in shaping the evolution of professional baseball. Its innovations, especially in terms of fan accessibility and player contracts, had a lasting impact on how the game was played and marketed. The AA helped to democratize baseball, bringing it closer to becoming America's national pastime.

The league's history is a testament to the dynamic nature of the sport in the late 19th century, showcasing the forces of competition and innovation that drove baseball forward. For modern fans and scholars, the AA provides rich historical context for understanding the business and culture of professional baseball and how the sport has continued to adapt and thrive over time.

Legendary Baseball Players of the 1800s
Baseball in the 1800s was a sport in evolution, and several key players helped popularize the game and transform it into America's national pastime. Their prowess on the field and sometimes flamboyant personalities off it captured public attention, laying the foundation for the baseball stars of the future.

Honus Wagner - One of the first superstars of baseball, Honus Wagner's career began in 1897. Known as "The Flying Dutchman" for his superb speed and German heritage, Wagner was a phenomenal hitter and a brilliant shortstop. He won eight batting titles, a record that stands to this day, and was one of the five inaugural inductees into the Baseball Hall of Fame in 1936.

Cy Young - The pitcher so excellent they named the award for the best pitcher after him, Cy Young's career spanned from 1890 to 1911. He still holds the MLB win record with 511, a testament to his dominance and durability. Young's incredible control over the ball and his ability to throw several different types of pitches made him a formidable opponent on the mound.

Cap Anson - Adrian "Cap" Anson was baseball's first true superstar. His career began in 1871 and spanned 27 years, during which he collected over 3,000 hits and batted .334. Anson was a charismatic player-manager for the Chicago White Stockings and was pivotal in the development of the National League.

King Kelly - Michael "King" Kelly, who played primarily for the Chicago White Stockings and the Boston Beaneaters, was one of the most colorful characters of the 19th century. A star player in the 1880s, he was known for his strategic batting and base-running skills. Kelly was also famous for his off-the-field antics and was one of the game's first matinee idols.

Ed Delahanty - Big Ed Delahanty was one of the most feared hitters of his era, batting over .400 three times during his career and finishing with a lifetime average of .346. His power and batting prowess were so well-known that they remain the subject of folklore. Tragically, his life and career ended prematurely when he fell into Niagara Falls in 1903.

Old Hoss Radbourn - Charles "Old Hoss" Radbourn had one of the most remarkable seasons ever for a pitcher in 1884, when he won an incredible 60 games for the Providence Grays. He was known for his competitiveness and durability, a true workhorse of his era.

Billy Hamilton - "Sliding Billy" was one of the game's great early base stealers, amassing over 900 stolen bases in his career, including a staggering 111 steals in 1889. Hamilton was also a tremendous hitter, with a career average of .344 and an on-base percentage of .455, numbers that underscore his skill at getting on base and wreaking havoc.

These players were more than just athletes; they were pioneers of baseball. They provided a template for the modern player, with their combination of skill, showmanship, and statistical prowess. Their legacies endure not only in the record books but in the fundamental ways the game is played and understood. Their contributions went beyond their individual accomplishments, as they helped turn a game into a professional sport and a national spectacle. The legends of these 19th-century baseball giants continue to be celebrated, and their stories are passed down through generations, preserving the rich history of baseball.

Baseball in 1900

The turn of the 20th century was a pivotal moment for baseball, marking the end of its formative years and the beginning of its maturation into America's national pastime. As the 1900s began, baseball was undergoing a transformation, fueled by a burgeoning American urban culture, technological advancements, and a nationalistic spirit that craved a uniquely American form of entertainment.

The National Game:

By 1900, baseball was already known as the "National Game" or "America's Pastime." It reflected the diverse aspirations and the democratic ethos of the United States. Having evolved from early bat-and-ball games like rounders, the version of baseball played in 1900 had become a spectator sport with professional players, commercial ballparks, and passionate fanbases.

Professional Leagues and Players:
Professionalism had taken root in baseball by the late 19th century, with the National League (NL) established in 1876 as a response to the disorganized and often rowdy state of the professional game. By 1900, the NL was the sole major league in operation following the folding of the American Association (AA) in 1891. However, this period also saw the consolidation of power among a group of NL team owners known as the "robber barons," who created a monopoly that controlled player contracts and wages.

The Birth of the American League:
The status quo of the NL faced a serious challenge in 1901 with the establishment of the American League (AL) by Ban Johnson. Johnson transformed what was originally a minor league, the Western League, into a rival major league. The AL introduced several changes that appealed to players and fans alike, including better pay for players and Sunday games, which were banned by the NL. The AL's defiance of the NL's reserve clause, which tied players to one team indefinitely, also allowed for greater player movement, attracting many star players from the NL.

Technological and Cultural Impacts:
The year 1900 saw baseball benefit from the era's technological innovations. The telegraph allowed scores and play-by-play accounts to be sent instantly across the

country, increasing the game's popularity and allowing for the rise of national sports journalism. The invention of the motion picture also gave fans their first glimpses of games and players in action, further embedding the sport into the American cultural fabric.

Social and Economic Factors:
Baseball in 1900 also mirrored the social and economic realities of the era. The Industrial Revolution had created a growing middle class with leisure time and disposable income, which helped to swell the ranks of baseball fans. Additionally, the influx of immigrants into the United States brought new fans to the sport, seeking to assimilate into American culture through the shared experience of baseball.

Race and Segregation:
However, not all was progressive in the baseball of 1900. The racial segregation of the sport reflected the prejudices of the time, with African American players barred from the major leagues, leading to the establishment of the Negro leagues in the coming decades. Despite this, baseball was a unifying force, with players of various ethnic backgrounds contributing to the diversity of the sport.

The Game Itself:
The game played in 1900 was different from today's sport in many ways. The dead-ball era, characterized by low-

scoring games and a focus on strategy over power, was in full swing. Pitchers like Cy Young, who would have a major award named after him, dominated the sport. The style of play involved more bunting, base-stealing, and hit-and-run tactics than the home-run-centric game we see today.

Legacy and Influence:
The year 1900 set the stage for a century of baseball that would see the sport become deeply integrated into the American consciousness. It would survive two World Wars, the Great Depression, and immense social change, emerging as a constant in American life.

Baseball in the year 1900 served as a microcosm of America itself, reflecting its challenges and aspirations. The establishment of the AL, the challenges to the NL's dominance, and the technological and social developments of the era all contributed to the game's growth.

1901: The Foundation of Major League Baseball
Baseball's popularity surged in the 19th century, laying the groundwork for what would become America's national pastime. Two leagues, the National League (NL) and the American Association (AA), competed for audiences, players, and profits. The NL, established in 1876, had sought to monopolize professional baseball

and held a dominant position after the AA folded in 1891. The NL then attempted to exert control over the game, its players, and its finances, including enforcing the reserve clause, which bound players to their teams indefinitely.

The NL's monopoly faced challenges as new entrants sought to capitalize on the sport's growing appeal. In 1894, Ban Johnson took over the minor Western League, renamed it the American League (AL), and sought to challenge the NL's dominance. Johnson saw an opportunity to create a league that would address the grievances of players and fans alike. He improved conditions for players, raised salaries, reduced the number of games played on the road, and took steps to eliminate rowdyism on the field and in the stands, improving the overall image of the game.

The AL declared itself a major league in 1900 and began placing teams in NL cities, encroaching directly on NL territory. Johnson strategically populated his league with stars by luring them away from the NL with the promise of higher pay and better working conditions. He also established teams in untapped markets that showed a strong appetite for professional baseball.

The creation of the AL and its open competition with the NL was pivotal. It culminated in what would be recognized as the official start of Major League Baseball in 1901. The move to declare the AL a major league was contentious, leading to what is known as the "baseball war," a period of intense rivalry characterized by legal battles and the fight for players, fans, and resources.

The AL's strategy was effective, and by 1901 it had teams in several major cities, including Boston, Chicago, and Philadelphia. The AL's Philadelphia Athletics, owned by Connie Mack, and the Chicago White Sox, owned by Charles Comiskey, were among the standout clubs, both of which would go on to play key roles in the league's history.

The rivalry between the two leagues intensified, but it also led to innovations, such as the introduction of the best-of-seven format for the World Series in 1905. However, the competition was not sustainable, and it became clear that a peace agreement was necessary. In 1903, the NL and AL came to a modus vivendi, recognizing each other's territorial rights, establishing a uniform players' contract, and creating the rules for what would become the modern World Series.

The establishment of MLB can be seen as an evolutionary process driven by the sport's internal dynamics and America's social and economic conditions. The start of MLB in 1901 marks not just the emergence of a new league but also the beginning of modern professional sports in America. It heralded an era of sports entertainment as a significant industry, complete with star players, passionate fans, and dynamic business moguls shaping the game's future.

The founding of MLB in 1901 was thus a confluence of entrepreneurial vision, player ambition, and public demand for a cleaner, more competitive, and entertaining sport. It set the stage for the development of baseball into an organized professional sport and laid the foundation for over a century of America's love affair with baseball, making it an essential chapter in the annals of American culture and sports history.

Legendary Baseball Players of the early 1900's
The first decade of the 20th century was a pivotal era for baseball, transitioning from the dead-ball era to a more modern form of the game. Several players stood out during this period, not only for their exceptional skills on the field but also for their ability to draw fans to the ballpark and increase the sport's popularity. Here are some notable figures including a couple of familiar players from the 1800's who also made a notable impact in the early 1900's:

Cy Young - Whose career spanned from the late 19th century into the early 20th, was a dominant pitcher known for his incredible endurance and pitching skill. Young's name is now synonymous with pitching excellence, thanks to the Cy Young Award. In 1901, he led the American League in wins, winning percentage, and strikeouts, setting the stage for a decade in which he would continue to excel.

Honus Wagner - also known as "The Flying Dutchman," was one of the era's most versatile and talented players. A shortstop for the Pittsburgh Pirates, Wagner won eight batting titles in his career and was known for his batting average, speed, and defensive abilities. His prowess during the 1900s helped the Pirates to their first World Series victory in 1909.

Christy Mathewson - or "Big Six," emerged as one of baseball's first true superstars in the early 20th century. Pitching for the New York Giants, Mathewson's mastery on the mound was unparalleled. He led the Giants to the 1905 World Series title, pitching three shutouts in six days, a feat that has become legendary in baseball lore.

Ty Cobb - known as "The Georgia Peach," began his career in 1905 with the Detroit Tigers and quickly became one of the game's most feared hitters. Cobb's aggressive style of play and competitiveness helped him win numerous batting titles and set numerous records, some of which stood for decades. His batting average over .400 in 1909 is a testament to his dominance at the plate.

Walter Johnson - though Walter Johnson's career took off more significantly in the 1910s, he made his debut in

1907 and showed early signs of the dominance that would define his career. Nicknamed "The Big Train" for his powerful fastball, Johnson became one of the most celebrated pitchers in baseball history, known for his strikeout records and his gentle demeanor off the field.

Eddie Collins - who started his career with the Philadelphia Athletics in 1906, was one of the era's best second basemen and a key figure in the Athletics' early success. Collins was known for his batting average, on-base percentage, and stolen bases, making him a threat both at the plate and on the bases.

Tristram E. Speaker - or "The Grey Eagle," made his major league debut in 1907 and is considered one of the best all-around players in baseball history. Speaker was renowned for his defensive skills in center field and his sharp batting eye, leading to a .345 career batting average and 3,514 hits. His intelligent play and leadership helped define the era's strategic approach to the game.

These players, among others, were instrumental in popularizing baseball in the United States. Their exploits on the field captivated fans and helped to elevate baseball to its status as America's pastime. Through their remarkable skills, competitive spirit, and sportsmanship, they left an indelible mark on the game that is still celebrated today.

The Most Influential Men Behind Baseball's Beginnings
The origins of baseball are a blend of myth and history, with various individuals contributing to its development and popularization.

Here are ten of the most influential figures in the early history of baseball:

Alexander Cartwright - Often credited as the "Father of Modern Baseball," Cartwright was instrumental in formalizing the game's first rules in 1845 as a member of the New York Knickerbocker Base Ball Club. His contributions include setting the diamond shape of the infield and establishing three-strikes as an out.

Henry Chadwick - A sportswriter and statistician, Chadwick is known as the "Father of Baseball" for his role in popularizing the game through his writings. He developed the box score, the batting average, and the earned run average, key statistics that remain fundamental to baseball today.

Albert Spalding - As a player, manager, and club president, Spalding championed the National League's formation in 1876. He later became a successful businessman, founding Spalding Sporting Goods, which helped standardize baseball equipment.

Harry Wright - Considered the first professional baseball manager, Wright organized the Cincinnati Red Stockings in 1869, baseball's first fully professional team. He introduced innovations such as signaling plays to players and is credited with many of the game's early strategic developments.

A.G. Mills - A former player and president of the National League, Mills chaired the Mills Commission, which in 1907 controversially credited Abner Doubleday with inventing baseball. Despite doubts about its accuracy, the commission's findings popularized the myth of baseball's purely American origins.

Ban Johnson - The founder and first president of the American League in 1901, Johnson was a driving force behind establishing the AL as a major league, leading to the modern two-league system and the World Series.

William Hulbert - As the second president of the National League, Hulbert is credited with saving baseball's first major league from collapse by enforcing strict professional standards and expelling teams that did not comply with league policies.

Candy Cummings - Although the claim is debated, Cummings is often credited with inventing the curveball in the early 1860s. This innovation changed pitching and batting strategies significantly.

Doc Adams - As a member of the Knickerbocker Base Ball Club, Adams is said to have created the position of shortstop and made significant contributions to the game's early rules and equipment, including the baseball itself.

Lipman Pike - One of baseball's first professional players, Pike was also one of its earliest Jewish stars, breaking cultural barriers in the sport. His career spanned from the 1860s into the 1880s, showcasing baseball's appeal to diverse communities.

These individuals, among others, played crucial roles in shaping baseball from a casual pastime into America's beloved national pastime. Their contributions to the rules, organization, strategy, and culture of the game laid the foundation for the sport as we know it today.

Made in the USA
Monee, IL
26 June 2024

e35a6762-7e36-4f52-a3f1-ecd2b93d92d2R01